max fax

SPACE

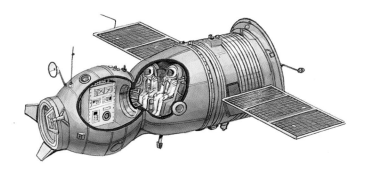

Max Fax:

SPACE

Also in this series:
Big Cats
Cars
Sharks

Cover photograph: Astronaut outside a spacecraft on the 1994 *Discovery* mission

Commissioning editor: Dereen Taylor
Series editor: Lisa Edwards
Book editor: Cath Senker
Designer: Luke Herriott
Subject consultant: Doug Millard, Science Museum
Language consultant: Wendy Cooling
Picture researcher: Shelley Noronha
Illustrator: Mark Bergin

Published in Great Britain in 2000
by Hodder Wayland, an imprint of Hodder Children's Books
First published in paperback 2001

A Catalogue record for this book is available from the British Library.

ISBN 0 7500 29749
Printed and bound in Italy by Eurografica S.p.a.

Hodder Children's Books
A division of Hodder Headline Limited
338 Euston Road, London NW1 3BH

SPACE

Tracey Blezard

HODDER
Wayland

an imprint of Hodder Children's Books

CONTENTS

WHAT'S OUT THERE?

Space is not empty. It contains things we can see, such as stars, and things we cannot see: gas, dust, black holes and X-rays. It is so vast that most of it has not been explored.

7,000 Milky Way stars can be seen with the naked eye.

The nine planets that orbit the Sun form our solar system. Many of these planets have one or more moons circling them. Also orbiting the Sun are comets and asteroids.

Pluto

Our solar system sits in a great swirl of stars called the Milky Way. This is our galaxy. It contains about 200 billion stars. In space there are millions of galaxies.

It seems ours may not be the only star system. One out of every ten stars could have planets. 51 Pegasi B was discovered in 1995.

51 Pegasi

51 Pegasi B

Jupiter

Earth

Illustration of a star 42 light-years away, 51 Pegasi. Compare the size of its planet, 51 Pegasi B, with Jupiter and Earth.

How far is our nearest star?

The nearest is the Sun, 150 million km from Earth.

Do stars die?

Yes, when they run out of gas. Bigger stars burn fuel more quickly than smaller ones, so they live shorter lives.

When will our Sun die?

It will burn for another 5 billion years.

Planets move around the Sun from West to East.

Our Sun is a star, a hot ball of gas. Other stars we see at night look different because they are much further away. The next closest star is Proxima Centauri, 4.3 light-years away.

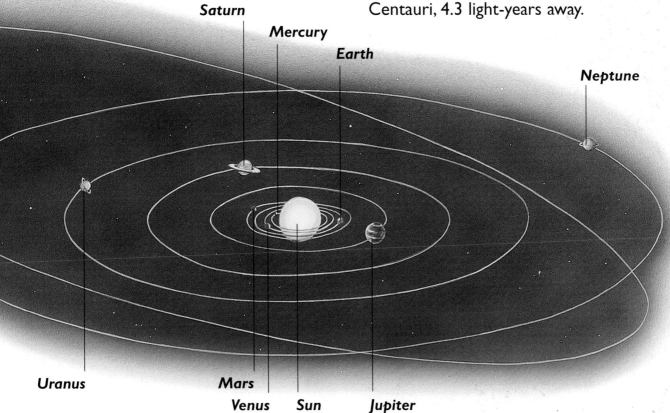

Saturn

Mercury

Earth

Neptune

Uranus

Mars

Venus

Sun

Jupiter

A Brief History

In ancient times, people saw space as a closed dome. The planets and stars hung from the top. The Earth was at the centre of the dome with the other planets orbiting it.

In 1609, Italian astronomer Galileo used the newly invented telescope to prove that the planets went round the Sun. The Earth was not at the centre of the universe.

An illustration from 1559 showing the Earth at the centre of the universe.

WATCH THIS SPACE

The Church hated Galileo's idea that the Earth was not the centre of the universe. He was locked in his house for eight years until his death in 1642.

In 1687, **English scientist** Sir Isaac Newton showed why the planets go round the Sun – gravity. Gravity pulls smaller things (the planets) towards bigger things (the Sun). Gravity also keeps people stuck to the ground on Earth!

In 1929, astronomer Edwin Hubble noticed that distant galaxies were moving away from each other. This proved that space is constantly growing.

1. Gas and dust clumped together to form the Sun.

2. The Sun sucked more gas and dust into a giant ring around it.

But how did the universe start? In 1965, Arno Penzias and Robert Wilson picked up radio-wave signals that came from a huge explosion in space about 14 billion years ago. This 'Big Bang' led to an expansion of the universe that continues to this day.

3. Some gas and dust broke away to form the planets.

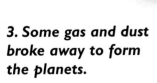

THE RACE TO THE MOON

In the '50s and '60s the space race was a battle between the super-powers: the USSR and the USA. In 1961, Soviet Yuri Gargarin was the first person in space.

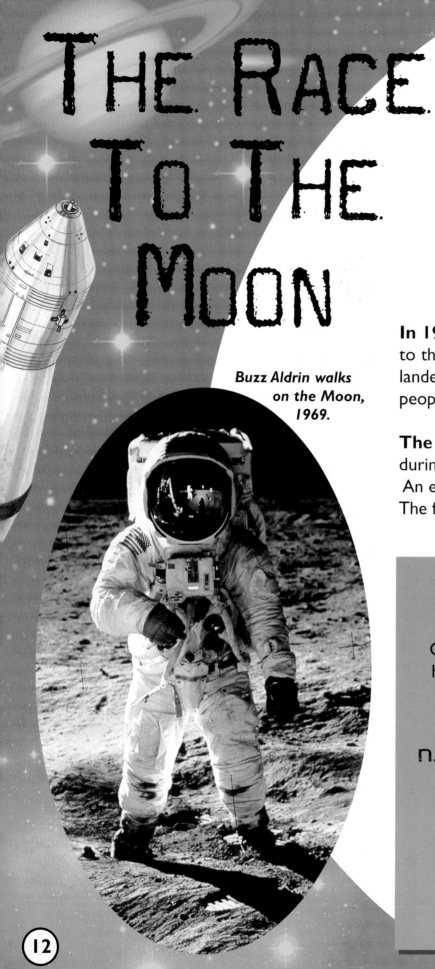

Buzz Aldrin walks on the Moon, 1969.

In 1959 a Soviet spacecraft crashed on to the Moon. In 1966 the USSR carefully landed a 100 kg craft. But neither ship had people aboard.

The US spacecraft, *Apollo 1*, exploded during a test on the launchpad in 1967. An electric spark had set light to the wiring. The fire killed the three astronauts inside.

Is there gravity on the Moon?

Only 20% of that on Earth, so even heavy objects, such as a car, can be picked up easily there.

Are days and nights the same as on Earth?

No. Each lasts 2 weeks at a time.

How many people have walked on the Moon?

12. The last was in 1972.

Apollo 11 **reached the Moon** in 1969. Neil Armstrong was the first to walk on the planet. He said it was 'one small step for man, one giant leap for mankind.'

1. Powerful rocket engines blasted Apollo 11 *into* the sky...

2. ...*then fell away. A smaller set of rockets and fuel tanks also dropped away.*

3. *A single engine powered the ship to the Moon. Astronauts landed in the Lunar Module.*

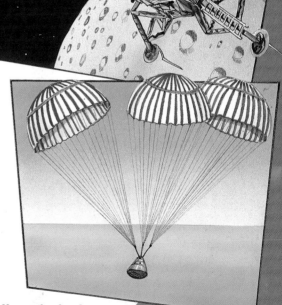

4. Apollo *splashed down to Earth and was picked up by navy ships.*

Valentina Tereshkova, the first woman in space, 1963.

SPACECRAFT AND PROBES

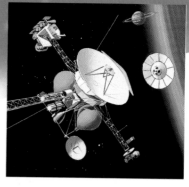

Cassini probe to Saturn, launched in 1997.

VentureStar, a re-usable rocket being built by NASA.

Unmanned spacecraft go deep into space, on missions too dangerous for people. They carry probes, which are lowered on to planets to collect information.

In the '60s, US probes pictured Mars from a distance. Soviet probe *Mars 3* landed in 1971, but its cameras failed. Other probes have crashed there or spun off into space.

United States

LOCKHEED MARTIN

VentureStar™

Manned Spacecraft

1. *In 1961, Mercury was big enough for one astronaut.*

2. *The Soviet Soyuz, launched in 1967, carried two or three people.*

3. *The 1980s Shuttle carried seven people. It landed like a plane.*

How far has a probe travelled?

Pioneer 10, the first craft to travel beyond our solar system in 1983, has travelled 8.5 billion km (1999).

Do probes return to Earth?

No. They either crash on to their target planet or drift off into space.

How many spacecraft have been sent to Mars?

31 US and Soviet launches since 1957.

In 1975 a Soviet probe photographed Venus for 53 minutes before it burnt up.

The US *Viking* probes of the 1970s searched for life on Mars, but the results were unclear. In 1997 cameras on a remote-controlled buggy showed the surface of Mars. Several missions failed in 1999, but attempts to explore Mars have continued.

Pluto, the furthest planet from us, has not yet been explored. A pair of small craft with a probe will leave for Pluto in 2001. The journey will take twelve years.

ASTRONAUT TRAINING

Nearly 400 people from many countries have gone into space. They include scientists, teachers and a prince. First they must pass months of tests, then complete one to two years of training.

Everything done in space is first practised on Earth using simulators – models of real spacecraft and equipment.

In space you are weightless. Astronauts train for this in a special plane. It makes sudden, sharp dives, giving short periods of weightlessness.

DID YOU KNOW?

● The Johnson Space Center, USA, has a swimming pool 13 m deep. It takes 29.55 million litres of water.

● The first Briton in space was Helen Sharman. She used to work for a sweet company developing ice-cream.

● Astronauts must learn to use over 600 switches on a spacecraft.

Water also gives astronauts a feeling of weightlessness when they are training.

'Zero gravity' inside the training plane.

Half the astronauts in space become space sick. They train for this by being strapped into a spinning chair.

How can I become an astronaut?

Do well at school. Study maths and science. Go to college.

How fit do I need to be?

Not 'super-fit', but healthy, and able to move quickly in an emergency.

How much do astronauts earn?

Between £25,000 and £50,000 a year.

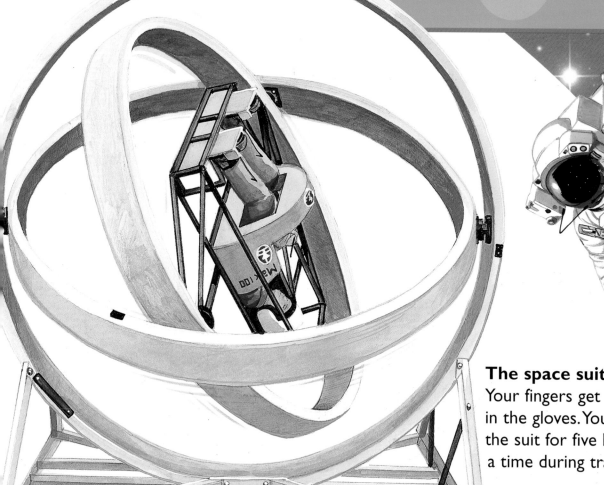

The space suit is stiff. Your fingers get bruised in the gloves. You wear the suit for five hours at a time during training.

An astronaut in the spinning chair forcing himself not to be sick.

LIVING IN SPACE

Putting together the international space station will take about 550 hours of work in space.

In 1971, Soviet astronauts stayed for 23 days in space. Their home was a tiny 'space station', 15 metres long, called *Salyut*. The last Soviet station, *Mir*, had visitors from around the world.

DID YOU KNOW?

- In space, without gravity pulling you down, you grow up to 7.4 mm taller.

- Astronauts take tablets to help them to go to the toilet regularly.

- Soviet astronaut Valery Polyakov holds the record for living in space. He spent 680 days in space – 439 of them on *Mir* during one trip.

By 2005, the USA, Russia, Canada, Europe and Japan will have finished building the first international space station. It will be a floating science laboratory, the size of a football field.

Everything in a spacecraft is specially made. Food must be sticky so it doesn't float away. Cups have lids with straws.

Astronauts float freely but Velcro keeps the equipment in place.

Exercise is important.

Without gravity, muscles become weak. After a year on *Mir*, some astronauts could not walk.

Astronauts strap themselves on to exercise machines.

Astronauts wash with a wet cloth. As there is no gravity, water sticks to them until they dry it off.

Astronauts in a space station.

DISASTER

73 seconds into its flight, **Challenger** *exploded.*

It costs $170 million to launch a rocket, so mistakes are expensive. But money is not the only problem. Mistakes can be deadly too.

Challenger *taking off.*

In 1967 engineers found 203 things wrong with a Soviet spaceship. It was launched, but crashed, killing the astronaut inside.

The air drained out of a Soviet spacecraft in 1971. It made a perfect automatic landing, but the three crew members inside were dead.

US space shuttle, *Challenger*, blew up in 1986. All seven crew members died. Hot gas had leaked on to the fuel tank. The result was a huge explosion.

WATCH THIS SPACE

Yuri Gargarin was the first person in space only because the planned first astronaut broke his leg!

The *Clipper Graham* Disaster

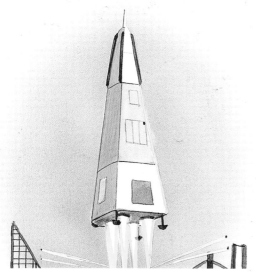

*1. In 1996, one of four landing legs jammed on the US **Clipper Graham** unmanned rocket.*

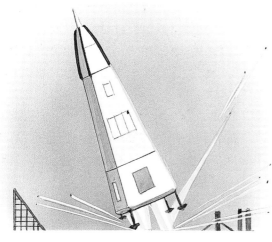

2. Three legs failed to hold it.

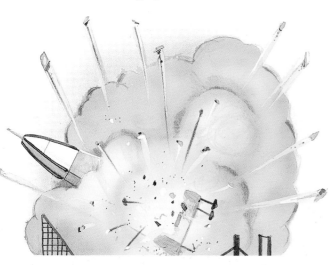

3. Crashing on to its side, it exploded.

Can spacecraft computers go wrong?

Yes. Then astronauts must steer the ship themselves.

When was the first death in space?

In 1957, when Laika the dog was put to sleep.

What was the worst space disaster?

190 people died when a Soviet rocket exploded on the ground in 1960.

On a lighter note... Waiting for take-off in 1961, Alan Shepherd peed in his suit. And in 1968, Frank Borman was sick over Apollo 8's instrument panels!

Laika was put to sleep after seven days in space.

BLACK HOLES

An artist's impression of a black hole.

Black holes form when large stars die. The holes are like monsters in space, swallowing everything that comes close. Once inside them, nothing can escape.

1. You are swept towards the centre of the black hole.

A black hole forms when a large star runs out of fuel. It shrinks and makes a deep well in space. At the bottom of the well is a point called a singularity. Here everything is squashed into nothing.

Black holes are black because no light shines out of them. They are invisible. Scientists know there is a black hole in space if they see stars being dragged around by an unseen force.

Inside a black hole the pull of gravity is super-strong. There is a point called the event horizon, which marks the point of no return. Go beyond here and you can never get out again.

Not all stars form black holes. Small stars become cold, hard rocks. Others may die in a huge explosion.

2. You start to stretch. Everything looks red.

3. Outside the hole, time seems to stop – inside, it's speeding up.

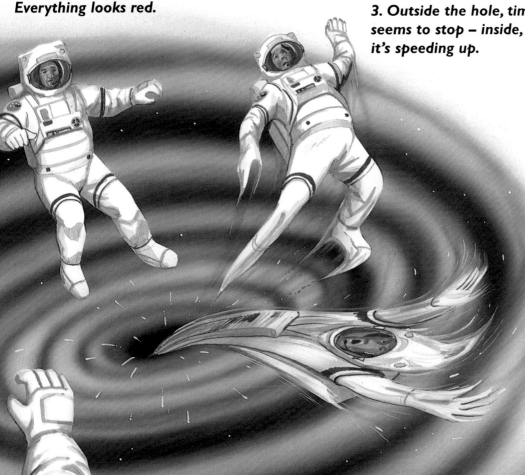

4. Gravity stretches you out – this is spaghettification. You disappear.

SPACE: THE FUTURE

Walking on the Moon? Living in space? One hundred years ago these were dreams. Now they are real. So what about our future?

Future probes to Mars will bring back samples of Martian rock to Earth. In 2013 two probes will land on Pluto. They will uncover the secrets of this icy planet and its moon, Charon, for the first time.

DID YOU KNOW?

- In the future, nuclear-powered rockets could be launched using lasers.

- Today, it would take our fastest spacecraft 80,000 years to reach Proxima Centauri.

- The chemicals needed to create life have been found in outer space, so life may exist elsewhere.

A remote-controlled rover explores Mars.

Mars is called the 'red planet' because of its red soil.

People may live in space – on the Moon or on floating space stations. They will grow plants and live in 'greenhouses'.

In the next twenty years astronauts will walk on Mars.

The frozen oceans of one of Jupiter's moons, Europa, will be explored. A robot will dig through the icy crust. It could find signs of life under the ice!

Re-usable rockets like the *VentureStar* will be built, making space exploration much cheaper. More people will go into space.

WATCH THIS SPACE

US President Dwight Eisenhower (1953–61) once said 'To spend $25 billion to go to the Moon is crazy.' But future presidents disagreed.

SPACE QUIZ

Can you find the right answers to these questions? They can all be found somewhere in this book. Check your answers on page 29.

1. How many planets go round the Sun?
a 7
b 9
c 11

2. Which of these stars is furthest away?
a 51 Pegasi
b The Sun
c Proxima Centauri

3. Who used a telescope to show the Earth went round the Sun?
a Galileo
b Newton
c Hubble

4. The first part of the solar system to be formed was:
a The Moon
b The Earth
c The Sun

5. Who was the first person in space?
a Neil Armstrong
b Valentina Tereshkova
c Yuri Gargarin

6. Which Apollo spacecraft landed on the Moon in 1969?
a Apollo 1
b Apollo 8
c Apollo 11

7. In 1963 Valentina Tereshkova was:

a The first woman in space

b The first person to die in space

c The first person to walk on the Moon

8. The furthest human beings have travelled into space is:

a Mars

b The Sun

c The Moon

9. What was *Mars 3*?

a A remote-controlled buggy

b The first probe to land on Mars

c A US spacecraft of the 1960s

10. Which sentence is true?

a All astronauts must be super-fit to go into space

b Space training lasts for 1–2 years

c Only Soviet and US astronauts have gone into space

11. What do astronauts practise in a giant swimming pool?

a Swimming

b Weightlessness

c Holding their breath

12. Which country had a space station called *Mir*?

a The USA

b The USSR

c China

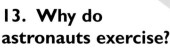

13. Why do astronauts exercise?

a They have time to kill

b Exercise machines generate power

c Muscles get weak in space

14 What is the name of Pluto's only moon?

a Europa

b 51 Pegasi B

c Charon

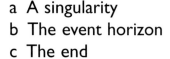

15. Which sentence is true?

a All stars become black holes when they die

b Small stars become black holes when they die

c Large stars become black holes when they die

16. What is the bottom of a black hole called?

a A singularity

b The event horizon

c The end

GLOSSARY

Asteroids Lumps of rock that go round the Sun. Most are between Mars and Jupiter. Some are the size of small planets.

Astronomer A scientist who studies the stars and planets, space, or the universe as a whole.

Comet A ball of ice and gas with a long tail of gas. Comets orbit the Sun.

Galaxy Group of millions or billions of stars, with gas and dust, held together by gravity.

Laser A powerful beam of light. In the future, lasers could be used to launch rockets.

Light-year The distance light can travel in a year – almost 10 million million kilometres.

Martian Something from Mars.

Moon-buggy An open-topped car used by astronauts on the Moon when collecting rocks and exploring.

NASA The US space agency: National Aeronautics and Space Administration.

Orbit To go round. For example, the Earth orbits the Sun.

Probe A spacecraft controlled from Earth, without astronauts on board.

Re-usable rocket A rocket that can go into space more than once.

Space shuttle A US spacecraft made in the 1980s. After going into space it could land like a plane back on Earth. It could be used again.

Space station A spacecraft where astronauts can live and work.

Speed of light Light travels at 300,000 km per second. In one second, light can go round the Earth seven times.

Star system A star with one or more planets orbiting it. Our star system is called the solar system, named after Sol, our sun.

Universe Everything in space.

Unmanned With no people on board.

Weightless Feeling that you don't weigh anything because there is no gravity.

Zero gravity Having no gravity to pull you down.

FINDING OUT MORE

Books

The Earth in Space by Peter Riley (Franklin Watts, 1998)

The Kingfisher Book of Space by Martin Redfern (Kingfisher, 1998)

The Marshall Children's Guide to Astronomy by Jacqueline Mitton & Simon Mitton (Marshall, 1998)

Space Encyclopedia by Heather Couper and Nigel Henbest (Dorling Kindersley, 1999)

Space, Stars, Planets & Space Craft by Sue Beckdale (Dorling Kindersley, 1998)

Space Stories That Really Happened by Andrew Donkin (Scholastic, 1999)

The Starry Sky: The Planets by Patrick Moore (Riverswift, 1994)

The Young Astronomer by Harry Ford (Dorling Kindersley, 1998)

CD-Rom

Starry Night (Sienna)

Video

The Story of the Total Eclipse: 11 August 1999 (Presenter Patrick Moore)

Websites

www.solarviews.com
www.maximov.com/iss
www.nasa.gov

Places to visit

Herstmonceux Science Centre and Observatory, Sussex
Tel: 01323 832731

Jodrell Bank Planetarium and Science Centre, Cheshire Tel: 01477 571339

The National Maritime Museum, Greenwich, London
Tel: 020 8858 4422

The Royal Observatory, Greenwich, London Tel: 020 8858 4422 (same as for the National Maritime Museum)

The Space Gallery at the Science Museum, London Tel: 020 7942 4000

Answers to quiz

1	b	5	c	9	b	13	c
2	a	6	c	10	b	14	c
3	a	7	a	11	b	15	c
4	c	8	c	12	b	16	a

INDEX

Page numbers in **bold** mean there is a picture on the page.

Picture acknowledgements

Genesis 14 (below), 19 (left), 20 (below); Getty Images 24; Popperfoto (Reuters) 17, 20 (above); Science Photo Library (Frank Zulla) 8, (Lynette Cook) 9, 10, (NASA) 12, (Novosti)13, (NASA) 14 (above), (NASA) 16, (NASA) 19 (right), (Novosti) 21, (Meham Kulyk) 22; Topham Picturepoint *Cover*; 18.